# Mary MacKillop
## TOUCHING OUR LIVES

### (CANONISATION EDITION)

# Mary MacKillop
## TOUCHING OUR LIVES

(CANONISATION EDITION)

Judith M Steer RSJ

ST PAULS

MARY MACKILLOP Touching Our Lives
Copyright: © 1996, 2008 by Judith M Steer RSJ

Illustrations © 2008 Dorothy Woodward RSJ

First published in 2008, reprinted 2009, 2010

National Library of Australia Cataloguing-in-Publication entry

| | |
|---|---|
| Author: | Steer, Judith M. |
| Title: | Mary MacKillop touching our lives / Judith M. Steer. |
| Edition: | Rev. ed. |
| ISBN: | 9781921472046 (pbk.) |
| Notes: | Includes index. |
| | Bibliography. |
| Subjects: | MacKillop, Mary, 1842-1909. |
| | Sisters of St. Joseph of the Sacred Heart– |
| | Biography. |
| | Nuns–Australia–Biography. |
| | Nuns–South Australia–Biography. |

Dewey Number: 271.97602

Published by
ST PAULS PUBLICATIONS
PO Box 906
Strathfield NSW 2135 Australia
http://www.stpauls.com.au

Cover design and internal layout by Kylie Prats

Printed in China by Everbest

ST PAULS PUBLICATIONS is an activity of the Priests and Brothers
of the Society of St Paul who place at the centre of their lives the
mission of evangelisation with the means of social communication.

# An Outstanding Figure

The settlers who came [to Australia] from Europe have always included a significant proportion of Catholics, and we may be justly proud of the contribution they have made to the building up of the nation, particularly in the fields of education and healthcare.

One of the most outstanding figures in this country's history is Blessed Mary MacKillop, at whose tomb I shall pray later this morning. I know that her perseverance in the face of adversity, her plea for justice on behalf of those unfairly treated and her practical example of holiness have become a source of inspiration for all Australians.

Generations have reason to be grateful to her and to the Sisters of Saint Joseph of the Sacred Heart and other religious congregations for the network of schools that they established here and for the witness of their consecrated life.

In today's more secular environment, the Catholic community continues to make an important contribution to national life, not only through education and healthcare, but especially by highlighting the spiritual dimension of the questions that feature prominently in contemporary debate.

*Pope Benedict XVI*
*Government House, Sydney*
*17 July, 2008*

# ACKNOWLEDGMENTS

For the revised edition of *Mary MacKillop: Touching Our Lives*, I acknowledge and thank the Sisters of St Joseph especially Marie Therese Foale, St Pauls Publications and many others for their help and support. I owe a debt of gratitude to my family and friends without whom I never could have written this little book. The idea of this small book came to me over the years, firstly, by being one of Mary MacKillop's 'daughters' as a Sister of St Joseph, then, from my thesis on religious biography and, finally, as I listened to the needs and desires of many visitors to the chapel and tomb of Mary MacKillop at North Sydney during the years around her beatification.

# CONTENTS

# INTRODUCTION

This biography is about the 'human' side of Mary MacKillop and how she touches the lives of people today in remarkable yet very ordinary ways. My aim is to make Mary MacKillop more accessible to people of all faiths, cultures and circumstances of life. My desire is that, as we reflect on the life of Mary MacKillop, we may absorb some of her fidelity, generosity, and freedom, and so become a source of healing and hope for others. This book focuses on Mary's response to life: how she managed trouble and suffering, how she grew as a person by knowing and accepting her own personal strengths and weaknesses, and how she trusted her loving God through it all.

This revised edition of *Mary MacKillop: Touching Our Lives* looks at the life experiences of Mary MacKillop using three aspects of the human condition: birth (or beginning experiences), death (or ending experiences) and creative action (or the experiences of new life). In these major life processes, or rites of passage, we discover her special gifts of faith (in her fidelity to the

Cross in her life), of hope (in her sense of dignity and freedom of spirit) and of love (in her generosity and compassion for people). In dealing with life's vicissitudes, she saw the positive in the negative, the possible in the impossible, and new birth and hope in failure and death. We can hope that, by reading this biography, we will be encouraged in our own troubles and suffering, and be challenged to new growth and deeper peace. Finally, we reflect on the life of Mary MacKillop and how we are challenged by the faithful, generous and free spirit of this special Australian, a real champion, our own Australian saint. 'She is a symbol of our Australian-ness.'[1]

*Judith M. Steer* RSJ

# UNDER THE
SOUTHERN CROSS

Australian! Heroine! Saint! What is the spirit pervading the life of Mary MacKillop that makes her so relevant and inspires us to emulate her today? Why is she so relevant? How are we inspired?

## AN INSPIRING LIFE

Mary MacKillop, a founding religious leader and colonial Australian, was beatified on Thursday 19 January 1995. In a ceremony presided over by Pope John Paul II in Sydney, Mary was recognised as 'Australia's Blessed One' – a saint for the Australian people. Then, at the canonisation on Sunday 17 October 2010, Mary was recognised as 'Australia's Holy One' – a saint for the whole world. Pope Benedict XVI presided over the ceremony at the Vatican.

Prior to the canonisation of our first Australian saint, all 'official' saints had to be 'imported', but now we have our own native-born saint, namely Mary MacKillop.[2] The qualities which make Mary MacKillop prominent as a Christian saint are not only her great deeds, her inventiveness, or her adaptability, but her unwavering belief in a loving God empowering her with a deep longing to give basic education and human dignity to the poor. She is the first to be recognised formally among the many unsung Australian saints who have made their own impact.

In writing for today's readers, authors are eager to turn their attention to the lives of women, to the poor, and to other groups omitted from past biographies. With regard to writings about Mary MacKillop, much has been published already on her life, work, and virtue.[3] More publications now are needed on how her spirituality is expressed, on the impact of her life, and on her relevance for today. This biography is an attempt to broaden and supplement existing writings about Mary MacKillop by focusing on her action in life's moments of mystery. Such moments of mystery may be similar to those in our own lives and reflecting on them may have a rich and positive impact for us. Simply by reading Mary's biography, many may experience a transforming effect in their lives.

## OUR LIVES

Reflecting on our own life journey urges us to think about the ultimate meaning of life, especially in moments in which the sense of the mystery of life is heightened.[4] Throughout life's journey we become aware of the life force: the mystery of birth and life, the mystery of suffering and death, the mystery of creative action in relationship and community. Birth experiences – like birth itself, as well as healing or recovery, the growth of a relationship or the start of a venture – herald beginnings. Death experiences, on the other hand, are like endings, for example, sickness, suffering, the break-up of a relationship, the ending of a venture, the diminution of life in some way, or death itself. Creative action however brings resurrection and renewal beyond birth and death, for example, the return of health, the refounding of a relationship, the rebuilding of a venture, or the regeneration of life in general in a new form. In such moments of birth, death and creative action we confront the mystery of God in our lives.[5]

Through such life forces[6] and moments of mystery, life is created and passed on from one generation to another.[7] Birth experiences bring us in touch with the source of life as gift. Death experiences help us realise the meaning of existence in letting go of life. By creative action in our relationships, we experience infinite love in creating community. Mary's engagement with experiences of birth, death and creative action empowered her to pass on faith and dignity to future generations. Through such common human experiences of birth, death and creativity, Mary responded to God in the essence of her being.

Looking at the stages in her life journey,[8] we may see how Mary expressed her identity in passing on faith, education and life skills to those in greatest need. The human strength or virtue that matched this particular stage in Mary MacKillop's life journey was perhaps her fidelity to her beliefs and her companions.[9] The life of Mary MacKillop reveals experiences that bring her in close contact with the traditional colonial Australian experience of hardship, privation and isolation, amidst mateship, in which wisdom is learned through suffering.[10] In Mary's life, her depth of wisdom is also learned through suffering, which, when combined with being faithful and generous and open to the 'Other', reveals the cutting edge of sainthood.[11]

⑬

Biographies that speak to us in our own contemporary situations are becoming increasingly popular. In Mary MacKillop's life we find parallels between aspects of her life and our own life experiences today. Major events in Mary MacKillop's own life and relationships point to the religious qualities that are needed in every way of life but, in particular, to our own lives. Such qualities are revealed in her experience of birth when she co-founded her new congregation in Penola, South Australia, in 1866; in her experience of death with her excommunication, 1871, her banishment from South Australia, 1883, and removal from leadership, 1885; and in her creative action, when she ensured the stabilisation of her young congregation by obtaining from Rome the (interim) Constitutions 1874 and (approved) Constitutions 1888, and when she eventually resumed the leadership of the congregation in 1899.

The life story of Mary MacKillop makes her a prominent figure in Australia's history of heroines and as such an authentic, 'true-blue' saint who is one of our own. Flowing out of her fidelity, generosity and freedom, was an ability to face the greatest of difficulties and sufferings in a prayerful spirit of peace and joy. Reflecting on these qualities and aspects of Mary MacKillop's life, people are drawn by her faithful trust in God, by her generous compassion towards those in need, and by her composure and freedom in following God's will for her in all the challenges of her life. The story of Mary MacKillop appeals to people who can resonate with her life when things get tough in their own.

# LIVING ON THE EDGE

Various vignettes from Mary MacKillop's life deal with aspects of her life story, including her family, childhood, youth, and adulthood. In these stages of her life course[12] and in the moments of mystery in her life experiences[13] we find the religious nature[14] of Mary's humanity.

It is amidst strengths and weak-nesses[15] highlighted in her religious biography that we find qualities of fidelity of mind, generosity of heart and freedom of spirit which became so pronounced as she responded to her special call and mission in life.

## MARY MACKILLOP'S LIFE

Mary's parents were from the highlands of Scotland. Her father, Alexander MacKillop, was born in 1812, and, as a young teenager, was sent to study for the priesthood in Rome. After six years of study, and being in poor health, he left the seminary before being admitted to ordination and returned to Scotland. Later, he decided to emigrate to Australia. Upon arrival in Sydney in 1838, Alexander obtained a good position of employment. Two years later, he met and married Mary's mother, Flora MacDonald, in Melbourne. Flora, also from the highlands of Scotland, had arrived in Australia a few months earlier. Initially, the couple lived in good circumstances in Brunswick Street, Fitzroy, Melbourne, where Mary was born on 15 January 1842.

Alexander and Flora had eight children in total: Mary, who carried much of the responsibility of the family while she was growing up; Maggie, who helped Mary with teaching but was often frail in health; John, who renovated Mary's first stable school in Penola, South Australia, prior to dying in his early twenties in New Zealand; Alex, who died as an infant; Annie, who supported Mary throughout her life and outlived all the family; Lexie, who entered the Good Shepherd Sisters but died only a few years later; Donald, who became a Jesuit priest and was Mary's confidant until his death; and Peter, the youngest, whom Mary encouraged especially in his studies at school in preparation for a good position in adult life.

## Childhood years

Alexander and Flora MacKillop were in a financially favourable position when they were first married, but circumstances soon changed this. Although very well educated, Alexander tended to be rash in his decisions and made regrettable mistakes. Flora, who also had received an education in her youth, did her best to manage the family affairs in her new country. Because of Alexander's mismanagement of the young family's financial affairs, they lost their home, were frequently on the move and often unable to pay the bills. This put considerable pressure on both Alexander and Flora, each being proud Highland Scots, as well as on all the children, especially Mary, the eldest.

As noted in a previous biography of Mary MacKillop, a significant event in the life of her family occurred after the birth of her brother, Donald, when Mary was in her twelfth year and their mother was ill: 'Noticing that the hired nurse was overfond of stimulants (Mary) promptly dismissed her, and, to her mother's bewilderment, took upon herself the duties of nurse as well as those of housekeeper.'[16]

In this event from childhood, Mary showed great competence. This happening marked the early tendency of Mary to take responsibility for the family when her mother found it difficult to manage and when her father was unable to provide for the family. Her father's inability in this regard caused all sorts of difficulties and brought constant strain on family relationships. While frequently being without support and having to depend on relatives, the family was often on the move and suffered many severe upsets. In short, Mary's early years were marked by poverty and hardship, sorrow and unhappiness. Her sense of responsibility for the welfare of her family at this early age was to be a marked influence on her adult life.

## Youth and early adult years

Mary cared for her family and became the main breadwinner in her mid teenage years. She held various positions of employment, initially in Sands and Kenny, stationers, then later as teacher and governess. Having succeeded in her teaching exams, Mary opened her own school for young ladies at Portland, in western Victoria. Later again, Mary went as governess for relatives in the Penola district of South Australia. It was here that her life's mission began most notably.

From the same chapter in the above-mentioned biography, another significant event occurred in Mary's youth – one which occurred during her employment with the stationers in Melbourne. When asked to show an international visitor around the plant, Mary did it with flare and professionalism. That evening, at a gathering of family and friends, she again met the visitor. But, instead of being acknowledged by him, she was snubbed. Such treatment was too much for her sensitive nature, so she left the party and went to her room in tears. All her friends, hearing how badly she had been treated, gave the visitor the same treatment and he soon had to leave the gathering. This incident highlights the sensitivity and vulnerability she had from the time of her youth and it seems to have set the way for her ever respectful treatment of others henceforth.

In her teens and as a young adult, Mary's sense of family identity, loyalty and fidelity were exemplified in her efforts to care for her younger sisters and brothers, and by her competent management of the entire family, year after year. Because she was so capable and so willing to keep the family out of debt and under the one roof, the family tended to depend on her for stability and security. She took responsibility for the family very seriously out of sheer need and from a strong sense of family loyalty and love.[17] These qualities were also evident in her interactions with others in all the various circumstances of her adult life and mission.

## Later adult years

Subsequently in adult life Mary expressed a similar pattern of dependability. Mary found herself responsible for all those Sisters who had come to join her congregation to teach and help the poor. With firm confidence, Mary drew the Sisters together in a bond of friendship and unity. With the exception of only a few, the Sisters responded with fond loyalty to her and a loving dedication to God and the poor.

From her earliest years, Mary wanted to dedicate herself to God. She had a sense that she was being called to work for God in a special way. It was this sense of 'vocation' that Mary gradually shared with Fr Julian Tenison Woods from the time she first met him, during her late teens. Mary had been well prepared for her work through the home education given her by her devout mother, and especially by her ex-seminarian father,[18] as well as by her attendance at school, at some stage.

In 1866, at the age of twenty-four, Mary started her congregation of teachers and carers who brought religion, education and support to Catholic working-class families in isolated and depressed areas in the Australasian colonies. Five years later, in 1871, while still in her twenties, Mary suffered the frightening injustice of excommunication from the church and the expulsion of almost half of her followers from their convents. But she had wisdom enough to sense that, in the end, all would turn out for the best. She obtained sound advice, followed her own conscience and lived from day to day in an unwavering belief in the loving providence of God. Then, at the age of thirty-two, she went to Rome seeking support for her congregation from Pope Pius IX. Later again, in 1874, Rome returned the interim Constitutions to Mary and her Sisters; these included some adjustments to the original Rule to suit Australian conditions.

In the following decade, however, further troubles befell Mary and some of her Sisters. In the shocking events of the Commission of Inquiry of 1883, Mary found herself banished from the Diocese of Adelaide. Then, in 1885, Mary was replaced as head of the congregation by Mother Bernard Walsh. It was only after 1888, with the final approbation of the Constitutions, that Mary and her Sisters had full canonical status as a religious congregation within the Catholic Church in Australia.[19] Finally, in 1899, after having been excluded from leading the congregation for fifteen years, Mary was elected as leader, a position she held until her death in 1909.

Throughout these later adulthood years, Mary's sense of identity, her innate loyalty and her remarkable fidelity were tested almost beyond human endurance. Such qualities had already been apparent in her living out of her mission earlier as a nun and as a founder of a new colonial religious congregation of women, but they were particularly tested in her role as religious leader of that congregation. Her sense of identity as a Catholic, as founder and as religious leader in adult life seems to parallel that of her earlier life in the developmental stages of her youth. In later years, her virtues of integrity and wisdom could be described as heroic, as evident in her efforts to help the poor and marginalised and to keep her Sisters together. Mary's mission was to help the Catholic people of colonial Australia come to a strong sense of their own identity as a church community.

## MARY MacKILLOP'S MISSION

Mary MacKillop can be classed among the hundreds of great colonial Australian women[20] who struggled – to a greater degree perhaps than did some colonial men – to achieve justice in schooling, social welfare and suffrage. Her time was an era in which great women in pioneer Australia were forming their identity[21] within Australian colonial society by educating the poor, claiming women's political rights and by providing welfare for women in need.

### Leadership

Under difficult pioneering conditions,[22] Mary MacKillop and Julian Tenison Woods founded a religious congregation of colonial women, the Sisters of St Joseph, in Penola, South Australia. Their aim was to provide religion, education and care for the poor working-class Catholic minority in nineteenth-century Australia[23] – a factor that was to contribute to the development of education for *all* children in Australia[24] *and* to the establishment of the Catholic system of education alongside the state system.[25] Mary had travelled through Europe, the British Isles and Ireland examining various religious congregations and Catholic schools. From this broadening experience she improved her own system of teaching which she had devised some years earlier to suit Australian conditions and needs.

Because her congregation was innovative, Mary needed all her inner strength to rebuff clerical attempts to take over the governing of her Sisterhood.[26] Strong leadership qualities were needed for her special mission to be planted, to survive and to flourish amidst the rugged circumstances of life in those times.

## Commitment

In her mission to bring the gospel to the poor and not just to those who could pay for an education, Mary MacKillop had to battle against the mindset of some of the Irish hierarchy of the church[27] when governments were establishing a system of education that was free, secular and compulsory. To fulfil her mission, and under the initial guidance of Fr Julian Tenison Woods, Mary went ahead without government aid and depended on the providence of God, as well as the generosity of people in general for the support of her teaching Sisters. In this way, those children whose parents were unable to pay school fees received a basic education while also being instructed in the faith. As a consequence of their work in isolated areas, the congregation of Sisters took on the responsibility of drawing together the Catholic communities around the schools located there. In this way, Catholic communities began to flourish even before parishes were formed or priests came to reside there. As a result, Mary's system of religion and education for the poor had a unique impact on Catholicism in colonial Australia.[28]

The quality of Mary MacKillop's religious leadership and commitment to mission explains much of the success of this Australian congregation in its mission. Equipped with her own experience of the prevailing living conditions and

despite the lack of any support at all in early Australian colonial life, Mary was able to train the first generation of her Sisters in a style of teaching and holiness adapted to robust colonial life.[29] This was seen by both Mary MacKillop and Julian Woods initially as their answer to the problem of the lack of religious education provided for Catholic children at that time.

## Partnership

Mary MacKillop's life's work is closely intertwined with that of Fr Julian Tenison Woods. While Fr Woods was stationed at Penola, Mary MacKillop – then a young woman – was a governess in the same area for the Camerons.[30] And while she was working there, she met Fr Woods, the parish priest of the far-flung Penola parish. He had the desire to help his scattered flock by setting up schools which imparted knowledge of religion and at the same time provided basic education for families who would otherwise have had no access to it. Further, Mary, who was a qualified teacher, expressed to Fr Woods her deep desire to serve God and the people around her. The coming together of the dreams of these two people sparked a whole new venture and the idea of the congregation was born. Thus the stable school at Penola became the first school in a wide network of schools, so making their dreams become a reality.

Julian Tenison Woods was to set Mary in the direction she was to follow for the rest of her life. With Julian as the instigator, Mary's life's work was the founding of a religious congregation of women who would devote themselves to teaching the children of poor families and to caring for women and orphans, the elderly and the destitute. Together, Julian and Mary founded a centralised Australian and New Zealand teaching congregation of women, the Sisters of St Joseph. Further, as well as founding this religious congregation, Julian travelled many miles on missionary activities throughout the Australian colonies spreading God's word wherever he could get an audience. Moreover, he travelled extensively throughout Australia and South-East Asia on geological and botanical research, writing many significant articles for important British scientific journals.[31]

Between such journeys and missionary activities, Julian was able to be in contact with the congregation which he co-founded with Mary MacKillop and especially with other smaller religious congregations which he had founded or helped to establish, for example, the Sisters of Perpetual Adoration, founded in Brisbane in 1874,[32] as well as the diocesan congregations of the Sisters of St Joseph in Australia and New Zealand.

∞

The lives of Mary MacKillop and Julian Tenison Woods each stretched over most of the second half of the nineteenth century. Mary, the teacher and religious leader, and Julian, the missionary and scientist, worked tirelessly for their church and country. Both were co-founders: Julian first, with the idea of the Sisters of St Joseph, then Mary, with the idea of becoming a nun. Their lives were spent mostly in the Australian colonies, as they together initiated what became an effective system of Catholic education caring for the poor throughout Australia and New Zealand.

In their ministry in colonial Australia, Mary and Julian exhibited qualities of inventiveness, initiative, tenacity and determination in the face of insurmountable opposition, a sense of justice for the underdog and an attitude of hope and optimism. How these two persons expressed these qualities in their lives is similar in some respects, but strikingly different in others. Julian could be described as the visionary and inspirer; Mary, the planner and pragmatist. With his extreme brilliance combined with his overflowing zeal, Julian tended to be flamboyant and intensely overcommitted. His missionary activity and scientific fieldwork could only be described as absolutely colossal. Mary, on the other hand, being more reflective and discerning perhaps, responded in a manner that was more balanced, level-headed and down-to-earth. Her educational vision was grounded in the ordinary and practical and she built on methods current at her time. However, the way the congregation operated was ahead of that time. During the early years of the MacKillop-Woods partnership, a very strong bond developed between them through their conversations and sharing of hopes and ideals. Evidence of their mutual care for, and admiration of, each other is found in their early letters.[33]

## Conflict and resolution

Genius and conflicts in the life of Julian Tenison Woods parallel inspiration and struggles in the life of Mary MacKillop. Virtues and strengths, as well as shortcomings and fragilities, highlight both the similarities and differences between these two religious figures. Julian Tenison Woods saw great qualities in Mary MacKillop and challenged her to use them in his plans for education and care of the poor. Mary MacKillop, on the other hand, was inspired by the genius and vision of Julian Tenison Woods – at least in the beginning. Later, she needed to go her own way. The mutually supportive partnership of Mary and Julian was to end fairly soon after the establishment of the congregation.

Initially, nevertheless, Julian acknowledged that Mary was the one who was called and most gifted to bring his vision to birth and maturity. Yet, sadly, so soon after the beginning of their ministry, and perhaps through misunderstanding, Julian changed his attitude and seemed to separate himself from Mary and the congregation they co-founded. Many reasons could be given to account for this apparent breakdown of the relationship. They came to differ in their views on how the Sisters were to keep the vow of poverty when Rome changed the Rule from requiring absolute poverty (by which the Sisters were to own nothing)[34] to a style of poverty more appropriate for Australian conditions (by which the Sisters were to own at least one piece of real property where they worked).[35] Julian felt betrayed and deeply hurt[36] because Mary had accepted this change in the expression of the vow of poverty which had been made by Rome. Later, they also disagreed over whether government of the congregation should be centralised or under the control of diocesan bishops. Even though Mary and Julian maintained a deep regard for one another all their lives, the rift in their partnership may never have really healed and it would have continued to have been a source of pain for them both. Nevertheless, some months before his death, when Mary asked if she could come and see him, Julian accepted her request. What was said at that final meeting of the two founders has not been recorded but Mary was able to convey his blessing to the Sisters of his first congregation.

## Mutuality and friendship

Throughout the years, Mary never forgot what Julian had done for her in setting her up for life. She always acknowledged and remembered with gratitude that Julian Tenison Woods was the one who had the creative dream for the church in his vast parish in the Australian bush. No matter what he did, Mary tried to make allowances for him. Even though Mary found it necessary to write to him, opposing some of his actions in very direct words, she never condemned him or cut herself off from him. When he was very ill, Mary was especially mindful of him. Yet, over the years, Julian seemed to remain aloof from both Mary and her Sisters. But, on the rare occasions when he did write to Mary, he always wrote with courtesy and respect, even though he did not agree with her point of view. Mary never understood why he acted as he did on some occasions but she remained true to herself and loyal to him throughout her life.

Mary always wanted her Sisters to remember Fr Woods with gratitude, in spite of the disagreements between them. About two years after his death, Mary, in a letter dated 4 March 1891, told her Sisters that it was her fond wish and hope that the building of the Mother House chapel at

North Sydney should be started and ' ... dedicated to the memory of our dear departed Father'. The dedication stone for the first Mother House chapel was laid later that year to commemorate the twenty-fifth anniversary of the founding of the congregation and it was dedicated to his memory.

## Mary's influence on others

The instances of giftedness together with shortcomings in the lives of both Mary MacKillop and Julian Tenison Woods make both persons more true to life. On one level, Julian found it difficult to work with others but he had a personal charm which was attractive to those around him. Mary, on the other hand, had an ease in relating to people but she struggled with her own weaknesses: her sensitivity and natural pride, and her inability to manage finances well.[37] Through all their virtues and shortcomings both Mary and Julian believed that God would see them through the worst situations. Today, when people reflect on the hardships, trials, tenacity and endurance evident in the lives of Mary and Julian, they may be encouraged perhaps in their own trouble and suffering and strengthened to cope with their cares and responsibilities. Thus the reading of the lives of Mary MacKillop and Julian Tenison Woods may be inspirational for people today, with the potential to be personally transforming.

Over the years, the impact of the Sisters of St Joseph in Australia and New Zealand, and, later, in Peru, Ireland, Scotland and elsewhere, has been quietly but strongly influential in building fidelity, generosity and freedom in the hearts of many people. With dedication similar to that of

Mary MacKillop and Julian Tenison Woods, the Sisters who joined them – and the people they helped – have become the spiritual progeny of them both; and the progeny of the following generation are those who have been nurtured to greater faith, greater hope and greater love. Today, the new progeny are the Sisters and all the groups and individuals associated in some way with Mary and Julian and their mission, as well as the many who are experiencing help and healing. Julian's impact on Mary MacKillop was through his ardent and unremitting apostolic zeal for mission and through his association with her in leadership and ministry. Mary's impact on us, in turn, has been through her fidelity, generosity and freedom in her mission, leadership and ministry; and, for many, Mary has become a heroine, mentor, model and friend.

# RITES OF PASSAGE

In nineteenth-century Australia, Mary MacKillop had a strong sense of the importance of passing on religion from one generation to another when she described vividly for the church authorities in Rome the conditions of faith in Australia. She knew the importance of not allowing whole generations of children to grow up in total ignorance of their religious beliefs and practices.

Religion has been viewed as a person's meeting with the 'Other' – with God – in the processes of the life journey: birth, death and creativity. Being religious in this sense is expressed in how a person in one generation manages such ever present faces of God in passing on life and spiritual values to the next generation. These powers are encountered in moments of mystery in the life journey by facing God incarnate in the depths of our being and in all our relationships. For Mary MacKillop, this meant meeting God within herself and reverencing God in others. Because of her belief in God incarnate in each of us, she faced the challenges of life with unshakeable faith, overflowing love and remarkable freedom.

These rites of passage of birth, death, and creative action – moments of mystery for all of us – are found in three segments of Mary's life's work: in the beginning of her congregation, in 1866; in the endings, with excommunication in 1871 and banishment in 1883; and in the regeneration of the congregation, with interim acceptance of the Rule by the highest church authority in 1874 and its definitive acceptance in 1888, and with the acceptance of Mary as leader once again in 1899.

A similar cycle of birth, death and creative action is observable in Mary's experiences of religious leadership: in her birth as leader of a congregation from 1866, in her death as leader of the congregation for fifteen years from 1885, and in her creative work as leader from 1899 to her death in 1909. A different example of the cycle though is illustrated in Mary's friendship with Julian Tenison Woods: in their initial partnership, in the breakdown of their relationship, and in Mary's efforts at reconciliation and Julian's apparent acceptance of this during his final illness.

These instances from Mary's life's journey illustrate the spiritual and psychosocial aspects of her experiences and define the overall religious quality of her life. Not only did she face potential dangers in life's moments of mystery, but she took advantage of the opportunities that presented themselves in these same moments of mystery. Generally, Mary lived life fully and dealt successfully with the life processes of birth, death and creative action but the constant struggle this entailed led to bodily diminution and sickness. Nevertheless, through her wholehearted engagement with these life processes, Mary grew to maturity and holiness in spirit.

## Birth Experiences

Mary MacKillop founded an innovative religious congregation in the church in 1866 to offset the ignorance, lack of faith formation and other social deficiencies of the time. Through the family struggles of her early life, Mary had come

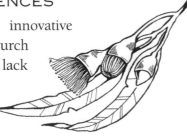

to appreciate the value of her Catholic faith and she could see round her the problems that arise from a lack of faith, education or care. This is why Mary, with Julian Tenison Woods as her director, set up a structure whereby she and her Sisters could live lives of dedication and prayer and, at the same time, bring knowledge of the faith, basic education and basic support to the people in isolated and depressed communities. Her passion for bringing faith through Catholic education to the working-class families of Australia and New Zealand was the driving force behind her work.

With the effort of bringing about the birth of the congregation, Mary brought new life to the people of her time. She wished to pass on those religious and moral values and life skills that would enable them to come to freedom, responsibility and fulfilment in their own lives. They in turn would be in a better position to engage their God-given power to pass on life and sound values to their offspring – the next generation. Within the social setting of her time, Mary could see the problems deriving from the lack of faith formation and from illiteracy. Her solution of a support system became a success on a national scale despite its small beginnings. Mary's generosity inspired others to be generous too. Many women joined the new congregation in those early years. This flow of generosity seems to have been part of the Australian character then – as now – and Mary was able to tap into that stream. She was the kind of leader who was able to be just one in the crowd yet was able to move mountains when it was seen as a matter of justice either to the members of her congregation or to others whom she served. As in the original Rule written by Fr Woods, Mary believed that if the Sisters were to work among the people, they were to make their home among the people.[38] Thus her helpers were mainly from the same level of society as those they served. Mary's kind of congregation suited these Australian conditions of ordinariness and was attractive to many ordinary Australian women.[39]

With the birth of a new faith generation through her congregation, Mary MacKillop expressed the human strength of love in the form of great generosity and compassion. The depth of generosity in her make-up may be detected in various small moments of birth within the broad sweep of her life. When she saw certain needs, she acted to remedy the situation at the root of the problem. With her birth experiences as religious leader in setting up a congregation of her own, she exercised power to give assistance where and how it was really needed. The qualities of generosity, compassion, inventiveness and initiative as seen in Mary MacKillop are not uncommon among Australians, who are known to exhibit these qualities when the need arises.[40] Thus through these birth experiences of her life, Mary MacKillop was one of the great pioneers of her time.

## DEATH EXPERIENCES

Mary MacKillop was wrongfully excommunicated from the church by Bishop Sheil in 1871, forced to leave Queensland in 1879, banished from the Adelaide Diocese by Bishop Reynolds in 1883, and dismissed from leadership at the mother house in Sydney by Cardinal Moran in 1885. In these instances and others, she suffered much at the hands of certain bishops. But although she was opposed by a few members of the hierarchy of the Australian church, she had the backing of others, as well as that of the Pope. She expressed her fidelity despite these death experiences by her enduring faith in God and by her loyalty to her Sisters and to the church generally. Strengthened through suffering and trusting in God's care of them, Mary and her Sisters were able to

continue their mission of education and care despite great odds against their successfully doing so.

Mary was firmly convinced about the need for central government of her congregation. At the time of her excommunication, when she and her Sisters were consequently suddenly put out of their convents around Adelaide, they had nowhere to live. However she was so convinced of this need for central government that she was prepared to withdraw her Sisters completely from dioceses where the conditions required for her congregation to operate were not being met. In the isolated and harsh Australian conditions which prevailed, she could see that this young group of women who joined her needed care and guidance for them to be effective[41] – hence the need for central government of the congregation by the Sisters themselves was a priority.

During the Adelaide excommunication crisis, Mary was helped and supported by many influential people, especially Mr Solomon and the relatives of the expelled Sisters, who made room for the Sisters when they had nowhere else to stay. Also, by writing to Rome, several lay people, including Father Woods' brother, James, played a part in preventing the suppression of the congregation. Later, in Queensland, when the Sisters were preparing to depart after losing the battle with Bishop James Quinn of Brisbane, the deeply concerned local townspeople tried to prevent their withdrawal.[42] In the instances of excommunication in Adelaide and withdrawal from Queensland, Mary's leadership was severely tested but she showed great tenacity, endurance and loyalty to her mission.

Despite the disruption to the new Sisterhood caused by the excommunication and the Sisterhood's partial dismissal in South Australia and the impossibility of negotiating with Bishops Matthew Quinn of Bathurst and James Quinn of Brisbane,[43] Mary remained firm. New openings were made with the blessing of Archbishop Vaughan in the Archdiocese of Sydney, where the congregation was greatly needed just at that time. With the withdrawal of the Sisters from Bathurst, Sr Hyacinth, with another Sister and eleven Irish postulants, remained and founded a new diocesan congregation under the bishop. When Mary withdrew the Sisters from Queensland, many of the places were taken over by the Sisters of Mercy, who had come to Brisbane in 1861, and who had been founded by Catherine McAuley a few decades earlier, in Ireland.

Mary experienced great trouble and suffering for her congregation during its development and during the years when she was kept out of leadership in favour of Mother Bernard Walsh, who seemed to be incompetent and to lack leadership qualities. As well as these major difficulties in her work, Mary endured great physical pain from various illnesses most of her life. Finally, she suffered severely from the effects of a stroke. In living through such death experiences in her life's journey, Mary drew on her own inner strength and loyalty, which have been regarded as worthy qualities in many Australians down the years.

The depth of her loyalty can be detected in how she responded to the moments of death within the broad spectrum of her life. She dealt with these death experiences by remaining faithful to her mission and by encouraging her Sisters to do the same. Like other women of her time, Mary showed great strength as a battler when she was excommunicated, forced to withdraw from Queensland, banished from South Australia and deposed as leader in New South Wales. In these death experiences, her fidelity was heroic to an extraordinary degree, reminiscent of the heroism and loyalty evoked in many great Australians when faced with critical moments of mystery in their own lives.

## CREATIVE ACTION

Mary MacKillop's creative action peaked in the aftermath of each traumatic event in the life of her congregation. After each major setback, she responded with all the charisma and power of her creative efforts to ensure an outcome of justice and to engender new beginnings. And with the approbation of the Constitutions of the congregation by Rome, initially in 1874 and finally in 1888, the congregation gained the church's full blessing on its work. The final approbation of the Constitutions by Rome in 1888 was one of the most important events for Mary and her Sisters. It provided security of tenure, freedom from interference at the local level and validation of their style of religious life. Another important event for the congregation was the full acceptance of the powers of the Constitutions by the Australian hierarchy with the election of Mary by the Sisters as the Mother-General of their choice, in 1899.

When Mary was able to take control of the leadership of the congregation again after the fifteen-year interruption, she used her creativity to renew the congregation. She set about correcting deficiencies which she perceived in the governance of the Sisters and in the quality of their own lives. She promoted the rights and freedoms of the Sisters by insisting that the Constitutions be followed not only by them themselves but that they be upheld by the clergy. She corrected difficulties, solved problems and eradicated faults firmly but with kindness, understanding and even a sense of humour. Through her creative action in all these areas, Mary gradually built up the morale of the Sisters. This role gave Mary the freedom to care for the Sisters' health and wellbeing and to encourage them in their endeavours.

Mary MacKillop's congregation was constituted to help ordinary people by providing faith formation, education and care. She had established a system of education in which even the poorest children could receive instruction in the faith and a basic education. In this endeavour, the Constitutions allowed for an adaptable lifestyle for the Sisters, either in crowded poor areas of the cities or in the sparsely populated and isolated country towns. Mary and her Sisters lived in tents or cottages with the people they served, enabling them to help the people in genuine need.

It was imperative that the Constitutions be fully approved by the church at the highest level – hence her journey to the Vatican to appeal in person to the Pope. When Mary arrived in Rome, Jesuit Fr Anderledy, who later became a Superior-General of the Jesuits, instructed Mary on vital issues which a founding religious leader would need to understand. This training proved to be of critical importance for Mary when she found herself and her congregation at loggerheads with some Irish bishops in the Australian colonies.[44] She fought

for what she believed was her responsibility to her congregation and the people she wanted to serve, in deference to
only the authorities in Rome.[45] But even here she appealed
initially against the decision of Pope Pius IX providing for the
ownership of property by the new congregation, although
she accepted that decision at once, when it was required to
be incorporated in the Constitutions. Throughout her life,
Mary acknowledged the ultimate authority of the Vatican;
for example, in her letter to her brother, Fr Donald MacKillop
SJ, many years later, she wrote, ' … and (I) do hope the
Sisters have not written anything that may be taken as want
of submission to Rome'.[46]

With the Constitutions of her congregation to
support her work, Mary was then free to follow her
mission to the poor of Australia and New Zealand. In her
leadership of the Sisters, she did not allow their work to
be hampered by convention or a mind-set which would
tend to overlook the needs of the Sisters who wished to
serve the real needs of the poor. An understanding of church
authority enabled Mary to be forthright with the hierarchy
while she retained her own integrity. Mary's patience,
perception and desire to follow what God wanted in her role
as leader under such difficult circumstances indicate her
inner strength and endurance. This is a good example of real
sanctity. She did not cling to her own will but freely followed
God in her life by remaining faithful to what she believed
God was asking of her in the approved Constitutions.
Traditionally, freedom is the mark of the Australian way of
life and character. The freedom of Mary MacKillop in her

creative action for the welfare of her Sisters and the poor portrays this distinctive Australian quality.[47]

## GROWTH

People were attracted by Mary's personal warmth, practical compassion and ordinariness. These qualities expressed the creative way she responded to God in dealing with the everyday experiences of her life. The impact of the life of Mary MacKillop is particularly important now with her beatification as Australia's first blessed and her canonisation as a universal saint. By knowing more deeply the mind and heart of this true-blue Australian, people may be challenged in the way they live their daily lives and be prepared to advance the cultural and religious transformation of Australia and the world.

In her life's journey of beginnings, endings and creative action, Mary MacKillop epitomises all that is best in the Australian character by way of loyalty, compassion and integrity. She is distinguished by her religious qualities of fidelity to her mission, generosity and freedom which, by the end of her life, had deepened to the point of heroic virtue – sanctity.

# 4

# STRANDS OF SANCTITY

This is Mary MacKillop – the woman, the saint, the Australian as seen in her life, relationships and leadership of her congregation. In both her strengths and her weaknesses we see quite clearly Mary's qualities of fidelity, generosity and freedom and we find a greater depth of meaning for our own lives. Mary MacKillop's qualities can be equated more precisely with the theological virtues of faith (in her fidelity), hope (in her freedom) and love (in her generosity) along with humility as the basic stance before God. We see how her spirituality is expressed in her lifestyle, in the impact of her life on others around her and in her relevance today.

## FAITH:
### FIDELITY AND LOYALTY

The charisma of Mary MacKillop in her life, relationships and leadership highlights the greatness of the first Australian saint. The special qualities of sanctity, expressed in the theological terms of faith, hope, love and humility,[48] are found conclusively in her joys and sufferings, and her strengths and weaknesses. When the path of life ran smoothly for her, Mary responded with prayer, gratitude and remembrance. When life became difficult, Mary responded with prayer, discernment and grit. The quality of Mary's response in any circumstance exemplified the humanness and holiness of her life. Whether in joy or sorrow, sickness or suffering, it seems that Mary endeavoured to respond positively, accepting each situation as a means for personal transformation.

Despite much physical suffering,[49] Mary MacKillop endured courageously and complained rarely, except to a few select people close to her. If she failed sometimes to accept and bear her sufferings patiently, she would begin again to take up her cross cheerfully. Through her openness to the opportunities of everyday life she responded to the call of the moment as best she could, whether in sickness, suffering or other troubles. Mary had a large share of the struggles of life and although she knew God provides generously and can be trusted, she did not escape being distraught at times. However, Mary used these life experiences as opportunities to follow the Christian way of union with Christ. She wrote, ' ... I felt that God wished me to keep under the Cross with Him ...'[50] – hence her preferred name, 'Mary of the Cross'.

Mary's positive stance, her sense of gratitude and her ability to bear all things patiently helped her cope with the vicissitudes of life. She was a model of fidelity and loyalty.

## HOPE:
### DIGNITY AND FREEDOM

A close look at Mary MacKillop as a person reveals a certain freedom of spirit in all aspects of life, whether great or small. Underlying her special strengths can be found a unique blend of humility and humour. A touch of humour in Mary's character enabled her to continue to move forward in trust when the odds seemed against her. A basic attitude of humility can be detected in Mary's words of encouragement to her Sisters, especially at the time of the excommunication. At the height of the trouble, one of the founding members of the Congregation received a letter from Mary:[51]

> Do not be surprised, dear Sister, when I tell you that I have been excommunicated by the Bishop tonight for non-compliance ...
>
> ... We have all good courage though. All my fear is lest any of my Sisters should act proudly, or say some unbecoming word. Oh, let us, if we cannot agree to what our poor dear old Bishop requires, at least be humble in the way we refuse ...

> ... I am firmly convinced that, should we refuse in a proud manner, God will never bring us together again. I need not ask you to have courage ...

Mary's simple humility and natural humour born of wisdom and suffering are the foundation for her sense of dignity and freedom of spirit.

## LOVE:
## GENEROSITY AND COMPASSION

The interpersonal relationships of Mary MacKillop were of an inspiring quality and reveal her beliefs about the people in her life and her attitude to them. Her compassionate nature was visible in her love and respect for the people she met, especially the children in her schools and orphanages, for the Sisters of her congregation and for the members of her own family. But it was the quality of her interactions with people of any class or station in life that earned her the respect of the poor and the compassion of the rich.

According to many of the Sisters who knew her, she was very homely and ordinary and had a natural love for people. She treated them all with acceptance and genuine love.[52] But, according to some of her early Sisters,[53] not everyone was able to see the love behind her words and deeds, even though she loved them all very much. Despite painful, unhappy situations in some of her relationships with others, Mary had the ability to sustain years of pressure and still be Christian in her treatment of everyone.

There are many stories about Mary's compassion and reverence for people from all walks of life – rich or poor;

Catholic, Jew or Protestant,[54] especially her friends, such as Emmanuel Solomon and Robert and Joanna Barr-Smith. Even though these friends of Mary were not Catholic, they helped her because they believed in what she was doing. Emmanuel Solomon gave Mary and her Sisters a place to stay rent-free for as long as was necessary after the excommunication. Joanna Barr-Smith often helped Mary overcome her financial difficulties, and when Mary died, it was Joanna who donated the grey marble tombstone which covers Mary's tomb in the convent chapel at Mount Street, North Sydney.[55]

Over the years, many children were helped and supported by Mary and the congregation she founded. Mary did not hesitate to help the poor, especially unhappy and troublesome children. A few years ago, for example, an elderly man[56] recalled his short but memorable meeting with Mary MacKillop in his youth, including the special encouragement she had given him and the self-respect she had stimulated. He had kept his school exercise book all these

years as a memento of this special meeting. More recently, another elderly man[57] recalled how Mary MacKillop had helped him when he was in one of her orphanages. He remembered how strong she and her Sisters were in feeding and educating all the destitute children. As orphans they were deemed to be of little worth by many, but Mary and her Sisters set them up for life, promoting good health and preparing them for productive jobs. As adults these men never forgot the good that Mary and her Sisters brought to them as children.

Many families also were helped by Mary MacKillop, who had the rare gift of accepting all people as she found them. Mary loved and respected everyone because she recognised the dignity of each person as a son or daughter of God and as redeemed by Christ.[58] Such love was expressed in her generosity and compassion for everyone.

## A MODEL FOR TODAY

Throughout her life, Mary MacKillop inspired her followers with devotion, courage, hope and enthusiasm. The various responsibilities she held and the way she worked through the difficulties she met enabled the quality of her religious leadership to be enhanced, demonstrating, in particular, her great vision and courage. As religious leader of her congregation, Mary MacKillop had to suffer much but she stood firm for her Sisters and the people they served.

Mary's courage and loyalty came to the fore when, as leader of her congregation, she was confronted with situations which seemed impossible to negotiate. However, her poor condition of health, combined with the difficulties she had with some high-ranking churchmen, dissipated Mary's energy,[59] and may have contributed to the chronic headaches which plagued her for more than half her life.[60] All through the crisis years of her congregation, she had to endure this chronic indisposition. But her retreat of 1897 was a time of great renewal of body and spirit. At this time – coming towards the end of a period during which another Sister was leading the congregation – there was a marked improvement in her health and a lifting of the mental anguish and heartache for the congregation, which, during this period, had lacked competent leadership.[61] Mary's natural great reserves of energy were her mainstay during these difficult times but ill health always took its toll. Today, people wonder at the fortitude of Mary MacKillop in all her struggles with those who were unsupportive, but there were many who held her in high regard throughout her life and supported her in any way they could.

In her ministry to the people, Mary, like her Scottish Highland parents, had strength of character, a capacity for endurance and loyalty to the faith.[62] The people she helped also shared this capacity for endurance, considering the situations in which she found them. Like the people she served, Mary was tough, strong-minded, tenacious and never gave up. By passing through these difficult experiences with courageous faith and love, Mary was able to lead others to new life and hope. Moreover, the Sisters who joined her were of a similar calibre and able to take on the example set for them by Mary. They suffered with her in various exigencies in their daily lives on mission, and were able to witness to those they served with a similar courageous loyalty, compassion and reverence for all. Today, Mary MacKillop is admired as one of the truly great religious leaders of the nineteenth century: a model of fidelity, generosity and freedom for today's troubled world.

## SANCTITY

A test of the genuineness of one's love is the quality of one's love for one's 'enemies'. It is significant that, throughout her letters, Mary MacKillop does not condemn any of those who opposed or wronged her. Her integrity was the key to her own inner journey, to all her personal relationships and to her style of religious leadership. With a deep compassion, Mary manifested the virtues of faith, hope and love in all her interactions, even in interactions with her apparent enemies. Her ability to inspire others with devotion and enthusiasm was obvious in her dealings with them. Her genuine love from the heart flowed naturally into the area of personal relationships – the sign of a truly great saint.

Mary MacKillop's experiences of births, deaths and creative action in her life's journey brought out the heroine and saint in her. In faith, Mary followed the Cross of Christ amidst all her pain and trouble, believing in God's loving presence in all. In hope, Mary brought freedom to the powerless through education and support, believing that God is the One to be trusted. In love, Mary brought dignity to the poor through her creative action, believing in God's loving providence to all.

Mary MacKillop's life is one of ordinary simplicity. She found it a joy to respond to God's invitations of love encapsulated in ordinary daily experience. She expressed her faith, hope, love and humility as fidelity, freedom, generosity and good humour in all her joys and sorrows, in all her strengths and weaknesses. Today, the church believes that Mary showed heroic virtue throughout her life and is worthy to be named a saint. She ' … conveyed the Christian Faith, not by exhortation, or discourse, or by polemic, but in herself. What they [the people of God] saw in her was a living faith, expressed in love'.[63]

The foundation of Mary's sanctity lies in her humility, expressed as humour born of wisdom learnt in suffering. Through common human experiences, Mary faced life's challenges with courageous faith, hope, love, humility and a sense of humour – qualities of a genuine saint. Generally, she did not take herself too seriously. An example of her humility and sense of humour is found in a letter already quoted in this chapter; it dates from the time of her excommunication: 'All my fear is lest any of my Sisters act proudly or say some unbecoming word.' A great Australian and a great saint, Mary MacKillop is a worthy model for people in contemporary society. She was tested through her life and survived the darkest nights of trouble and suffering. Australians today are searching for a model and anchor in life to help them through all kinds of impossible situations and personal difficulties. Mary MacKillop is a saint for ordinary Australians today.

On the global scene, Mary MacKillop is an inspiration to all in any need, especially in times of human tragedy and injustice experienced by whole nations or groups of people. Not only is she an Australian for Australians and has been called upon for her prayers by many Australians past and present, but she is needed by people throughout the world as they search for dignity, freedom and peace. This search concerns the field of work of a universal saint. Gradually the influence of Mary MacKillop is being recognised universally by people in need from many countries of the world. Through her prayers of intercession to God, she can make a difference in our lives.

The sanctity of Mary MacKillop may be found in the humility, humour, wisdom and suffering of her life and relationships. Its primary aspect is how she lived solely for God in serving others with a loving heart. With a mix of humility and humour in her strengths and weaknesses, she embodies in her life all that it means to be an Australian saint. Faithful, generous and free, through her birth experiences, death experiences and creative action, Mary MacKillop is at once saintly and Australian.

## 5

# A CHAMPION
# AND HER CHALLENGE

Australians love champions, especially for their vision and courage. Yet what is most appealing about the first Australian saint is how ordinary and homely she was, how sensitive she was to God in her life, how accepting and respectful of others, how forgiving, yet how extraordinary. In many ways, Mary MacKillop is an icon for Australia: a heroine and a saint.

## A CHAMPION

As a committed Christian, Mary MacKillop responded to the needs of the poor by cutting through convention and established structures and mind-sets of the church. She was not a radical, revolutionary, or reformer but she did what many other committed Christian women were doing in colonial Australia. But what makes Mary MacKillop extraordinary is the way she lived her life. She was a person who became a saint by her fidelity, generosity and freedom as she pushed the ruling limits of church and society. Fired by faith, hope and love she drew on all her resources to support and empower the poor, even in the face of her own humiliation and failure. Naturally broad-minded, Mary was simple, ordinary and down-to-earth, and friend to both rich and poor.

Some biographers of Mary MacKillop note the struggle she had as the champion of the oppressed by emphasising the 'suffering saint' aspect, while other writers highlight the ordinariness and goodness of this great Australian woman. The sanctity of Mary MacKillop, according to one author, touches on the larrikin quality admired by all Australians in their heroes and heroines – saints and sinners alike – a quality especially appealing in Mary MacKillop.[64] According to another writer, 'the experience of the woman, Mary MacKillop and of her "daughters" continues to captivate the imagination of contemporary women and men'.[65] Readers now are convinced of her relevance as an Australian saint and are encouraged by her distinctive contribution to the Australian way of life. To many, she is a real champion.

## TOUCHING OUR LIVES TODAY

Many people are floundering today amid difficulties on many sides: in building and maintaining marriage relationships, in raising a family, in searching for employment or in facing retrenchment, eviction from their homes, failure in business or troubles on the land; and families are touched by yet other problems: sickness, addiction, grief and suicide. The impact of these problems on individual persons and on their loved ones is devastating. There is no easy way out. Life has to be faced and transformed.

The story of struggle in Mary MacKillop's life captures the attention of many in similarly difficult circumstances. To those who know her and have felt her impact on their lives, she is regarded as one of them; or rather, they regard themselves as one of hers. Despite her ordinariness, Mary MacKillop stands out as a model, mentor and saint. She expresses the essence of Australian sanctity through her fidelity, generosity and freedom and provides us with a model of common human goodness made  accessible to everyone – a goodness seen especially in her relationships and spirituality.[66]

When people come to know the inner spirit of Mary MacKillop, they learn to love and forgive through her example.[67] They see how she tackled problems created by the unfair traditions, structures and mind-sets of her time, and are perhaps strengthened and encouraged in their own struggles and sufferings. Mary is recognised by many ordinary people from various creeds, cultures, and walks of life as one who has gone before them and shown the way. They find in her an example of survival, joy and hope in the midst of trouble, crisis and failure.

Mary MacKillop, Australian heroine and saint, fits the pattern of the 'fair dinkum' Australian and the 'fair dinkum' saint. She is 'true-blue'. There is no doubt that she is a model for today's world. In her body she carried the cross of sickness, pain and suffering. In her heart she carried the cross of misunderstanding, hurt and failure. But in her spirit she carried the power of resurrection through her love and forgiveness, creating a better world for the dignity of all. For many in Australia – and elsewhere – Mary is touching their lives with her example of fairness, courage and forgiveness.

## OUR CHALLENGE

What challenges us today is to see our lives reflected in that of Mary MacKillop. In almost every aspect of our troubles and sufferings, we can find a parallel in Mary's life, a life modelled on Christ. The details of her life's difficulties may be different from our own but the essence of them is the same. It is surprising how one person can have such a variety of troubles packed into one life and yet this is how it was for Mary MacKillop.

The core of Mary MacKillop's challenge to us is for us to see how courageously she faced her many different trials and tribulations, and how fully she responded to the whole-of-life process of birth-death-resurrection. People find hope, encouragement and strength in their own lives when they reflect on similar experiences in Mary's. They can see their own struggles reflected in hers and are challenged by how she responded to similar experiences. Just as Mary MacKillop did before them, so too can they change the negative into the positive, the impossible into the possible, and failure and death into new life and hope.

As spiritual model for our times, Mary MacKillop shines in the ordinariness of her life and in the depth of her spirituality.

She has been recognised already as having a religious impact equal to that of any other great religious leader of the English-speaking world.[68] Her greatness is apparent in her life and in the many letters she wrote – letters which contain a wealth of spiritual nourishment of real benefit for present and future generations. Mary's exceptional example of fidelity, generosity and freedom makes crucial for our times the melding of an authentic Australian spirituality.

Saint! Heroine! Australian! In being all these, Mary MacKillop lived from day to day in faith, hope and love through all the moments of mystery in life common to everyone. Ordinary people can identify with her in the simple aspects of everyday living yet her life as described in religious biography makes the application of these titles to her very appropriate today. Mary MacKillop is truly a symbol of our Australian-ness – 'Australia's Holy One'.[69]

# CHRONOLOGY
## OF MARY MACKILLOP'S LIFE[70]

## Mary's parents

1812  Birth of Mary's father, Alexander MacKillop, in Scotland

1816  Birth of Mary's mother, Flora MacDonald, also in Scotland

1825  Alexander enters Scots College, Rome, to study for the priesthood but leaves six years later, before ordination

1838  Alexander MacKillop arrives in Sydney, Australia

1840  Flora MacDonald arrives in Melbourne, Australia

## Birth and early childhood

1840  Marriage of Alexander and Flora in Melbourne

1841  Flora wears a relic of the true Cross during pregnancy

1842  15 January: Mary MacKillop born in Fitzroy, Melbourne

1842  April: financial difficulties: the family home is sold and the family begins living with various relatives

## Teenage and young adulthood

1858  Mary begins work as a shop assistant with Sands and Kenny

1860 Mary begins employment as a governess at Penola Station, South Australia, where she first meets Father Julian Woods

1863 Appointed to a denominational school in Portland, Victoria

1864 Opens her own School for Young Ladies at Portland

## Beginning of her life's work

1866 Mary opens a stable school at Penola, South Australia; beginning of congregation

1867 Father Julian draws up first Rule of the congregation

1867 15 August: Mary MacKillop professes her first vows

1868 Dr Sheil approves the Rule drawn up by Fr Tenison Woods

1868 19 December: death of Mary's father, Alexander, in Victoria

1869 31 December: Sisters of St Joseph arrive in Brisbane

## Excommunication and expulsion

1870 Trouble in Adelaide with Mary away in Queensland

1871 127 Sisters and 34 schools in South Australia at this time

1871 April/May: Mary returns to South Australia and begins visiting the convents

1871 22 September: Bishop Sheil excommunicates Mary 47 Sisters expelled from the Adelaide convents

1872 23 February: excommunication lifted by Bishop Sheil

1872 1 March: death of Bishop Sheil

## Papal approval for congregation

1873  Mary goes to Rome to obtain formal approval for her congregation. While waiting, Mary visits convents and schools in France and Germany, and goes to England, Scotland and Ireland to gather support

1874  21 April, from Rome: Mary receives revised interim Rule from Pope Pius IX

1875  December: after three years in Bathurst, a separate diocesan congregation begins under Bishop M. Quinn

1879  March: beginning of withdrawal of Sisters from Queensland

1880  Foundations established in Sydney Archdiocese and Armidale Diocese

1883  November: first New Zealand foundation, at Temuka

## Deposed as leader and banished

1883  17 November: Mother Mary deposed by Bishop Reynolds and ordered to leave Adelaide

1885  October: Mother Bernard appointed as leader by Cardinal Moran

1886  30 May: Mary's Mother, Flora, drowns off New South Wales coast

1887  Sisters arrive in Western Australia

1888  25 July: final papal approval as a regular congregation with mother house in Sydney made distinct from diocesan congregations

1889  7 October: death of Fr Woods, in Sydney

1889  First foundation in Victoria, at Numurkah

1891  December: Mary seriously ill in Melbourne

## Return to leadership

1899  10 January: Mother Mary elected by the Sisters as General, 28 votes to 2, after the death of Mother Bernard the previous year

1899  Plans to go to Jesuit Aboriginal mission at Daly River but flooded out

1900  Sisters return to Queensland, at Clermont, in Rockhampton Diocese

1900  Mother Mary's *Account of the History of the Congregation* (1866-1900)

1901  February: Mary presents 'Garland of St Joseph'

1902  11 May: Mary suffers a stroke in New Zealand

1903  15 June: Mary presents her *Life of Fr Woods*

## Death, beatification and canonisation

1909  8 August: death of Mother Mary MacKillop in Sydney. Funeral Mass at St Mary's Church, North Sydney, then buried at Gore Hill

1913  Mary MacKillop Memorial Chapel built in Mount Street, North Sydney

1914  29 January: Mary's body reinterred in the chapel

1993  20 December: Mary's body removed to the new shrine in the chapel

1995  19 January: Mary MacKillop beatified by Pope John Paul II in Sydney

2009  8 August: centenary of the death of Mary MacKillop

2010  17 October: Mary canonised by Pope Benedict XVI at the Vatican

# BIBLIOGRAPHY

Archives of the Sisters of St Joseph, North Sydney: diaries, letters, documents, records, resource material on Mary MacKillop, Julian Tenison Woods and the Sisters of St Joseph.

Abbott, Walter M. *Documents of Vatican II*. London: Chapman, 1966.

Boland, T. P. *Quiet Women*. Deception Bay, Qld: Refulgence, c. 1974.

Breward, Ian. *Australia: 'The Most Godless Place Under Heaven'?* Adelaide, SA: Lutheran Publishing House, 1988.

Burford, Kathleen E. *Unfurrowed Fields: A Josephite Story: NSW, 1872-1972*. North Sydney: St Joseph's Convent, 1991.

Campion, Edmund. *Australian Catholics*. Ringwood, Vic: Viking, 1987.

Costello, Emmet P. *Saints: Popular and Relevant*. Strathfield, NSW: St Pauls Publications, 1994.

Cuskelly, James. Unpublished homily celebrating the 75th anniversary of the death of Mary MacKillop, St Stephen's Cathedral, Brisbane, August, 1984.

Dunne, Clare. *Mary MacKillop – No Plaster Saint: A Pioneering Woman for Our Time*. Crows Nest, NSW: Australian Broadcasting Commission, 1991.

Earley, Ciaran. 'Moments of Mystery'. *Word Magazine*, February 1994, 22-3.

Eliade, Mircea. *The Sacred and the Profane*. New York: Harcourt, 1959.

Eliade, Mircea and Joseph Kitagawa, eds. *Encyclopedia of Religion*, Vol. 6. New York: Macmillan. 1986-. S.v. 'Homo Religiosus', by Gregory D. Alles.

Erikson, Erik H. *Childhood and Society*. New York: W. W. Norton, 1963 and 1985.

_____. 'Identity and the Life Cycle: Selected Papers'. *Psychological Issues* 1, no. 1 (1959) 1-171.

_____. *Insight and Responsibility: Lectures on the Ethical Implications of Psychoanalytic Insight*. New York: W. W. Norton, 1964.

Feehan, Victor and Ann MacDonell. *In Search of Alexander MacKillop* 2nd rev. edn. Sydney: St Joseph Publications, 1994.

Foale, Marie Therese. *The Josephite Story: The Sisters of St Joseph: Their Foundation and Early History 1866-1893*. Sydney: St Joseph's Generalate, 1989.

Fogarty, Ronald. *Catholic Education in Australia 1806-1950*. 2 Vols. Melbourne, Vic: Melbourne University Press, 1959.

Gilroy, Ann L. 'Mary MacKillop and the Challenge to Her Daughters'. *Australasian Catholic Record* 72, no. 1 (January 1995) 61-72.

Gardiner, Paul. (New ed.) *An Extraordinary Australian – Mary MacKillop*. North Sydney: Trustees of the Sisters of St Joseph, 2007.

_____. *Positio Prot. N. 704 Sydney Cause of Canonisation of the Servant of God Mary of the Cross MacKillop (1842-1909)*.

Unpublished document produced for the Congregation for the Causes of the Saints in 3 Vols. Rome, 1989.

Gorman, Clem. *The Larrikin Streak: Australian Writers Look at the Legend.* Sydney: Macmillan, 1990. S.v. 'Mary MacKillop – Saintly Larrikin', by Max Harris.

Goodman, Robert. 'History of Education in Australia'. Unpublished lectures, External Studies Department, The University of Queensland, c. 1960s.

Hutch, Richard A. 'Biography as a Reliquary'. *Soundings* 76, no. 4 (Winter 1993) 467-85.

_____. 'Reading Lives to Live: Mortality, Introspection, and the Soteriological Impulse'. *Biography* 17, no. 2 (1994) 125-43.

_____. 'Strategic Irony and Lytton Strachey's Contribution to Biography'. *Biography* 11, no. 1 (Winter 1988) 1-15.

Joyce, Martina. 'The Sisters of St Joseph in Queensland: Beginnings'. *Proceedings: Brisbane Catholic Historical Society* 3 (1992) 35-50.

Keane, William. 'The Cause of Mother Mary MacKillop'. *The Australasian Catholic Record* 29, no. 2 (April, 1952) 101-16.

Lyne, Daniel. *Mary MacKillop: Spirituality and Charisms.* North Sydney: St Joseph's Generalate, 1982.

_____. *Mary MacKillop: Made in Australia.* Strathfield, NSW: St Pauls Publications, 2009.

MacDonell, Ann, and Robert MacFarlane. 'Cille Choirill Brae Lochaber Inverness-Shire' 3rd edn. Fort William, Scotland, 1995.

McEntee, Walter. 'The Sisters of St Joseph of the Sacred Heart in Queensland, 1869-1880'. Unpublished BA thesis, The University of Queensland, 1978. Microfiche.

McLeod, Bill. *'I Remember … Mary MacKillop. Reflections of Bill McLeod.'* Interview by Caroline Jones. A Transmission Media Production, 1993. Videocassette.

Modystack, William, *Mary MacKillop: A Woman Before Her Time*. Adelaide: Rigby, 1982.

O'Brien, Felicity. *Called to Love: Mary MacKillop*. Strathfield, NSW: St Pauls Publications, 1993.

O'Brien, Leslie. *Mary MacKillop Unveiled*. North Blackburn, Vic: CollinsDove, 1995.

O'Donovan, Denis, chairman. 'Departure of the Sisters of St Joseph'. *The Brisbane Courier*, Wednesday, 17 December 1879.

O'Farrell, Patrick. *The Catholic Church and Community: An Australian History* 3rd edn. New South Wales University Press, 1992.

O'Neill, George. *Life of Mother Mary of the Cross (MacKillop) (1842-1909): Foundress of the (Australian) Sisters of St Joseph*. Sydney: Pellegrini, 1931.

_____. *Life of the Reverend Julian Edmund Tenison Woods (1832-1889)*. Sydney: Pellegrini, 1929.

O'Sullivan, Colleen. 'What Does Sainthood Mean for Australian Catholics Today?' *Australasian Catholic Record* 72, no. 1 (January 1995) 53-60.

Pickering, Evelyn. 'Pastoral Vision of Mother Mary MacKillop'. Unpublished papers. Pastoral Conference, North Sydney, c 1980s.

Pickering, Evelyn, and Anne Marie Power, eds. *Resource*

*Material from the Archives of the Sisters of St Joseph of the Sacred Heart*, 10 Issues. Archives of the Sisters of St Joseph of the Sacred Heart, North Sydney, 1976-1988.

Power, Anne Marie. 'We Are Her People: Mary MacKillop – Woman of Australia'. Unpublished pamphlet. North Sydney, 1982.

_____. *Sisters of St Joseph of the Sacred Heart: New Zealand Story, 1883-1983*. Auckland, NZ: Sisters of St Joseph, 1983.

Press, Margaret M. *Julian Tenison Woods: 'Father Founder'*. Strathfield, NSW: St Pauls Publications, 2004.

Radi, Heather, ed. *200 Australian Women: A Redress Anthology*. Broadway, NSW: Women's Redress Press, c. 1988. S.v. 'Caroline Chisholm (1808-1877) immigrants' friend', by Heather Radi; S.v. 'Mary MacKillop (1842-1909) religious', by Marie Therese Foale.

Ryan, Joan. *A Seed is Sown ... A History of the Sisters of St Joseph of the Sacred Heart 1890-1920*. East Burwood, Vic: Advent Business Forms, 1992.

Staub-Staude, Lorna. *The Anatomy of a Saint: Inspired by the Life and Work of Mary MacKillop*. Naracoorte, SA: Lorna Staub-Staude. c. 1992.

Steer, Judith M. 'Mary MacKillop: A Biographical Study of Australian Sainthood'. Unpublished MA(StTh) thesis. The University of Queensland, 1994.

_____. 'Select Bibliography: Publications on Mary MacKillop'. *Australasian Catholic Record* 72, no. 1 (January 1995) 73-80.

Summers, Anne. *Damned Whores and God's Police: The*

*Colonisation of Women in Australia*. rev. edn. Ringwood, Vic: Penguin, 1994.

Thompson, Zita. 'Australia's Holy One'. Words and Music. Gabriel Doheny. Accompaniment. *A Saint for Today* Hymns composed by Margaret Cusack RSJ and Zita Thompson RSJ to celebrate the Canonisation of Mary MacKillop. Trustees of the Sisters of St Joseph, 2010.

Thornhill, John. *Making Australia: Exploring Our National Conversation*. Newtown, NSW: Millennium Books, 1995.

Thorpe, Osmund. *Mary MacKillop*. 3rd rev. edn. North Sydney: The Generalate, Sisters of St Joseph of the Sacred Heart, 1994.

Tierney, P. Lucy. 'A Feminine Strand in the Weaving of an Australian Identity'. Unpublished essay; part of coursework MTh at Catholic Theological Union, Sydney, 1996.

Tranter, Janice. 'Fr Julian Tenison Woods: His Role as Founder of the Sisters of St Joseph at Lochinvar'. *Journal of the Australian Catholic Historical Society* 12 (1990) 45-58.

Turner, Naomi. *Catholics in Australia*. 2 Vols. North Blacktown, Vic: Collins Dove, 1992.

White, Patricia. 'An Icon in Australia'. Unpublished poem. Penola, SA. c. 1992.

Wilson, Andrew, ed. *Mary MacKillop: A Tribute*. Leichhardt, NSW: Honeysett Press, in association with the Mary MacKillop Secretariat, 1995.

Woodward, Kenneth L. *Making Saints: How the Catholic Church Determines Who Becomes a Saint, Who Doesn't and Why*. New York: Simon & Schuster, 1990.

# FURTHER READING

Barnes, Helen. *The Cross: An Australian Journey*. Strathfield: St Pauls Publications, 2008

Cresp, Mary. *In the Spirit of Joseph*. North Sydney: Sisters of St Joseph of the Sacred Heart, 2005.

Cuskelly, Eugene James. *Mary MacKillop, A Spiritual Model for All*. Strathfield, NSW: St Pauls Publications, 2010.

Kane, Sue and Leo. *The Little Brown Book: Mary MacKillop's Spirituality in Our Everyday Lives*. Strathfield, NSW: St Pauls Publications, 2009.

McCreanor, Sheila J., ed. *Mary MacKillop & Flora: Correspondence between Mary MacKillop and Her Mother, Flora McDonald MacKillop*. North Sydney: Sisters of St Joseph of the Sacred Heart, 2004.

McCreanor, Sheila J., ed. *Mary MacKillop in Challenging Times, 1883-1899: A Collection of Letters*. North Sydney: Sisters of St Joseph of the Sacred Heart, 2006.

McCreanor, Sheila J., ed. *Mary MacKillop on Mission to her Last Breath – Correspondence about the foundation of the Sisters of St Joseph in Aotearoa New Zealand and Mary's final years 1881-1909*. North Sydney: Sisters of St Joseph of the Sacred Heart, 2006.

McKenna, Margaret M. *With Grateful Hearts! Mary MacKillop and the Sisters of St Joseph in Queensland 1870-1970*. North Sydney, Sisters of St Joseph, 2009.

O'Sullivan, Colleen. *The Gift of Mary MacKillop*. Mulgrave, Vic: John Garrett Publishing, 2007.

Snudden, Patricia. *Imaging Mary MacKillop: With Whisperings From Mary.* Strathfield, NSW: St Pauls Publications, 2010.

Steer, Judith. *Saint Mary MacKillop: Friend of Jesus.* Illustrations by Dorothy Woodward. Strathfield, NSW: St Pauls Publications, 2010.

Wicks, Pauline. *God Will Take Care of Us All: A Spirituality of Mary MacKillop.* Strathfield, NSW: St Pauls Publications, 2009.

Wicks, Pauline. *Mary MacKillop: Inspiration for Today.* Marrickville: Lindwall and Ward, 2007.

# NOTES

1   Patricia White, *An Icon for Australia* (poem).

2   William Keane, 'The Cause of Mother Mary MacKillop', *The Australasian Catholic Record* 79, no. 2 (April 1952) 101-16.

3   See Judith M. Steer, 'Select Bibliography: Publications on Mary MacKillop', *The Australasian Catholic Record* 72, no. 1 (January 1995) 73-80.

4   Ciaran Earley, 'Moments of Mystery', *The Word* (February 1994) 22-3.

5   Richard A. Hutch, 'Reading Lives to Live: Mortality, Introspection, and the Soteriological Impulse', *Biography* 17, no. 2 (1994) 125-43.

6   Concerning natality, mortality and sexuality (creative acts), see Hutch, 'Reading Lives to Live', 125-43.

7   Richard A. Hutch, 'Biography as a Reliquary', *Soundings* 76, no. 4 (Winter 1993) 467-85.

8   Erik Erikson, *Childhood and Society* (New York: W. W. Norton, 1963 and 1985) 247-74.

9   Erik Erikson, 'Human Strength and the Cycle of Generations', in *Insight and Responsibility: Lectures on the Ethical Implications of Psychoanalytic Insight* (New York: W. W. Norton, 1964) 111-57.

10  John Thornhill, *Making Australia: Exploring Our National Conversation* (Newtown, New South Wales: Millennium Books, 1992) 101.

11  See Kenneth L. Woodward, *Making Saints: How the Catholic Church Determines Who Becomes a Saint, Who Doesn't, and Why* (New York: Simon and Schuster, 1990) 392.

12  See Erik H. Erikson, 'Erikson's Eight Psychosocial Themes',

*Psychological Issues* 1, no. 1 (1959) 120.

13  For 'religious' biography, see Hutch, 'Reading Lives to Live', 125-43.

14  Mircea Eliade and Joseph M. Kitagawa, eds, *The Encyclopedia of Religion*, Vol. 6 (New York: Macmillan, 1986- ), s.v. 'Homo Religiosus' by Gregory D. Alles. For a discussion of the religious foundation of the human, see Mircea Eliade, 'Human Existence and Sanctified Life', in *The Sacred and the Profane* (New York: Harcourt, 1959) 162-213.

15  Richard A. Hutch, 'Strategic Irony and Lytton Strachey's Contribution to Biography', *Biography* 11, no. 1 (Winter 1988) 1-15.

16  George O'Neill, *Life of Mother Mary of the Cross (MacKillop) (1842-1909): Foundress of the (Australian) Sisters of St Joseph* (Sydney: Pellegrini, 1931) 11.

17  William Modystack, *Mary MacKillop: A Woman Before Her Time* (Adelaide, SA: Rigby, 1982) 11-18.

18  Osmund Thorpe, *Mary MacKillop*. 3rd rev. edn. (North Sydney: The Generalate, Sisters of St Joseph of the Sacred Heart, 1994) 12-16.

19  Paul Gardiner, *An Extraordinary Australian: Mary MacKillop* (Newtown, NSW: E.J. Dwyer; David Ell Press, 1993) 12-16.

20  See Marie Therese Foale, 'Mary MacKillop', in Heather Radi, ed., *200 Australian Women: A Redress Anthology* (Broadway, NSW: Women's Redress Press, c. 1988) 40-2. See neighbouring entries in the same monograph concerning other great Australian colonial women who also served needy people in various ways.

21  Anne Summers, 'God's Police', in *Damned Whores and God's Police* rev. edn (Ringwood, Vic: Penguin, 1994) 337-62.

22   See Patrick O'Farrell, ed., *Documents in Australian Catholic History*, Vol. 1 (London: Geoffrey Chapman, 1969) 413.

23   Naomi Turner, *Catholics in Australia: A Social History*, Vol. 1 (North Blackburn, Vic: Collins Dove, 1992) 132.

24   Robert Goodman, 'History of Education in Australia' (unpublished lecture notes; St Lucia, Brisbane: The University of Queensland, External Studies Department, c. 1960s).

25   Ronald Fogarty, *Catholic Education in Australia 1806-1950*, Vol. 2 (Melbourne: Melbourne University Press, 1959) 257.

26   Kathleen E. Burford, *Unfurrowed Fields* (North Sydney: St Joseph's Convent, 1991) 11ff, 25ff. See also Felicity O'Brien, *Called To Love* (Strathfield, NSW: St Pauls, 1993) 101.

27   Patrick O'Farrell, *The Catholic Church and Community: An Australian History*, 3rd edn (Kensington, NSW: NSW University Press, 1992) 171-75.

28   Walter McEntee, 'The Sisters of St Joseph of the Sacred Heart in Queensland 1869-1980' (unpublished BA thesis; St Lucia, Brisbane: The University of Queensland, 1978) 3, 4. Microfiche.

29   Edmund Campion, *Australian Catholics* (Ringwood, Vic: Viking, 1987) 45-50.

30   Lorna Staub-Straude, *The Anatomy of a Saint: Inspired by the Life and the Work of Mary MacKillop* (Naracoote, SA: Lorna Staub-Straude, c. 1992) 1-16.

31   See O'Neill, *Life of the Reverend Julian Edmund Tenison Woods (1832-1889)* (Sydney, NSW: Pelligrini, 1929) 399-406, concerning the 155 articles for journals, newspapers, etc. These writings still have relevance more than a century after Woods published them.

32  For congregations of men and women founded by Julian
    Tenison Woods, see T. P. Boland, *Quiet Women* (Deception
    Bay, Qld: Refulgence, c. 1974) 150-66.

33  See 'Mary and Julian: Their Letters 1862-1868,' Sisters of
    St Joseph, 1989.

34  Mary appealed against, but then accepted, the final
    decision of Rome on the matter. See Sisters of St Joseph,
    eds, *Constitutions of the Sisters of St Joseph of the Most Sacred
    Heart of Jesus,* 1874 and 1986. See also Sisters of St Joseph,
    eds, *Companion to the Constitutions* (Sisters of St Joseph,
    1988).

35  See O'Neill, *Life of the Reverend Julian*, 268, for the letter
    from Mary to the Queensland Provincial.

36  Janice Tranter, 'Fr. Julian Tenison Woods: His Role as
    Founder of the Sisters of Saint Joseph, Lochinvar, NSW,'
    *Journal of the Australian Catholic Historical Society* 12 (1990)
    445-58. See also Felicity O'Brien, *Called to Love*, 58, 87.

37  Lesley O'Brien, *Mary MacKillop Unveiled* (North Blackburn,
    Vic: CollinsDove, 1995) 266-7. (See note 54)

38  Anne Marie Power, 'We Are Her People: Mary MacKillop
    – Woman of Australia' (unpublished pamphlet, North
    Sydney, 1982) 31.

39  Marie Therese Foale, *The Josephite Story: The Sisters of St
    Joseph: Their Early History 1866-93* (Sydney: St Joseph's
    Generalate, 1989) 202-3, 222-3.

40  Bishop James Cuskelly, Homily commemorating the 75th
    anniversary of the death of Mary MacKillop (Brisbane: St
    Stephen's Cathedral, August 1984).

41  See references to central government in the primary
    documents: 'Observations on the Rule' (1873), 'The
    Necessity for the Institute' (1873), and 'Reasons for a
    General Superior for Our Institute' (1873), in Evelyn

Pickering and Anne Marie Power, eds, *Resource Material No. 3, 1980/1984* (North Sydney: Archives of the Sisters of St Joseph).

42 O'Donovan, Denis (chairman), 'Departure of the Sisters of St Joseph', *Brisbane Courier*, Wednesday, 17 December 1879.

43 See Margaret Press, *Julian Tenison Woods: 'Father Founder'* rev. edn (North Blackburn, Vic: Collins Dove, 1994) 144-56, 170-93. See also Martina Joyce, 'The Sisters of St Joseph in Queensland: Beginnings 1870-1880', *Proceedings* (Brisbane Catholic Historical Society) 3 (1992) 35-50.

44 Gardiner, *An Extraordinary Australian*, 177. Some Irish bishops created problems for Mary MacKillop's congregation by interfering in areas of responsibility relating to the congregation concerning which they had no authority to act.

45 See 'Form of Petition to Pope Pius IX from Mother Mary of the Cross in Daniel Lyne', in *Mary MacKillop: Spirituality and Charisms* (Sydney: St Joseph's Generalate, 1983) 139-43.

46 Letter of Mary MacKillop to Donald MacKillop, SJ, 9 December 1897.

47 See P. Lucy Tierney, 'A Feminine Strand in the Weaving of an Australian Identity' (unpublished essay; part of coursework MTh; Sydney: Catholic Theological Union, 1996).

48 Paul Gardiner, *Positio: Congregation for the Causes of the Saints Prot. N. 704 Sydney Causes of Canonisation of the Servant of God Mary of the Cross MacKillop (1842-1909)*, Rome, 1989, Vol. 3, 4-58. See also Walter M. Abbott, 'Lumen Gentium', *Documents of Vatican II* (London: Chapman, 1966) nn. 39-42.

49 Mary became seriously ill when in Victoria. See Joan Ryan,

*A Seed is Sown* ...*A History of the Sisters of St Joseph of the Sacred Heart* (East Burwood, Vic: Advent Business Forms, 1992) 92. And Mary suffered a stroke in New Zealand; see Anne Marie Power, *Sisters of St Joseph of the Sacred Heart: New Zealand Story 1883-1983* (Auckland, NZ: Sisters of St Joseph of the Sacred Heart, 1983) 254-7.

50  See Letter of Mary MacKillop to Donald, 29 December 1897.

51  Letter of Mary MacKillop to Sr Francis Xavier Amsinck, 21 September 1871.

52  See examples of this in the Declaration of Witnesses required for the Process of Canonisation 1916-1925 (North Sydney: Archives of the Sisters of St Joseph).

53  Foale, *Josephite Story*, 192-3.

54  Clare Dunne, *Mary MacKillop – No Plaster Saint: A Pioneering Woman for Our Time* (Crows Nest, NSW: ABC Enterprises, for the Australian Broadcasting Corporation, 1991) 70.

55  O'Brien, *Mary MacKillop Unveiled*, 225, 263-5. In 1996, the birth details – 'Born in Melbourne, January 15th 1842' – were added.

56  Oral history (North Sydney: Archives of the Sisters of St Joseph).

57  See Caroline Jones' interview of Bill McLeod in the video *I Remember ... Mary MacKillop* (Transmission Media Production, 1993). In January 1994, McLeod died, aged 103.

58  Emmet P. Costello, *Saints: Popular and Relevant* (Strathfield, NSW: St Pauls, 1994) 69-78.

59  See Foale, *Josephite Story*, 193.

60  There are many instances in which Mary mentions being ill. See her Diary, 14 January, 1896. All she could write was: 'Very ill all day'.

61 Mother Bernard, who had been kept in the position of leadership for fifteen years, lacked appropriate leadership qualities. See Burford, *Unfurrowed Fields*, 51-72.

62 Anne Frater, 'A Message from Scotland', in Geoffrey Hull, *Building the Kingdom: Mary MacKillop and Social Justice*. ACSJC Occasional Paper no. 22. (North Blackburn, Vic: HarperCollins Publishers, 1995) 36-8. See also Ann MacDonell and Robert MacFarlane, 'Cille Choirill Brae Lochaber Inverness-Shire' 3rd edn (Fort William, Scotland, 1995) 8, art.24; and Victor Feehan and Ann MacDonell, *In Search of Alexander MacKillop* 2nd rev. edn (Sydney: St Joseph Publications, 1994) 24-5.

63 Gardiner, *Positio*, Vol. 3, 115.

64 See Max Harris, 'Saintly Larrikin', in Clem Gorman, ed., *Larrikin Streak: Australian Writers Look at the Legend* (Sydney: Macmillan, 1990) 177-88.

65 Ann L. Gilroy, 'Mary MacKillop and the Challenge to Her Daughters,' *The Australasian Catholic Record* 72, no. 1 (January 1995) 61-72.

66 Judith M Steer, 'Mary MacKillop: A Biographical Study of Australian Sainthood' (unpublished MA(StTh) thesis; St Lucia, Brisbane: The University of Queensland, 1994) 77-81.

67 Colleen O'Sullivan, 'What Does Sainthood Mean for Australian Catholics Today?' *The Australasian Catholic Record* 72, no. 1 (January 1995) 53-60.

68 Ian Breward, *Australia: 'The Most Godless Place Under Heaven'?* (Adelaide: Lutheran Publishing House, 1988) 93.

69 Zita Thompson, *Australia's Holy One* (song).

70 Modystack, *Mary MacKillop*, 271-9.

# INDEX